FIRST 50
JAZZ STANDARDS
YOU SHOULD PLAY ON GUITAR

ISBN 978-1-4950-7668-8

HAL•LEONARD®
7777 W. BLUEMOUND RD. P.O. BOX 13819 MILWAUKEE, WI 53213

Visit Hal Leonard Online at
www.halleonard.com

GUITAR NOTATION LEGEND

THE MUSICAL STAFF shows pitches and rhythms and is divided by bar lines into measures. Pitches are named after the first seven letters of the alphabet.

TABLATURE graphically represents the guitar fingerboard. Each horizontal line represents a string, and each number represents a fret.

4th string, 2nd fret — 1st & 2nd strings open, played together — open D chord

HALF-STEP BEND: Strike the note and bend up 1/2 step.

WHOLE-STEP BEND: Strike the note and bend up one step.

GRACE NOTE BEND: Strike the note and immediately bend up as indicated.

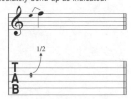

SLIGHT (MICROTONE) BEND: Strike the note and bend up 1/4 step.

BEND AND RELEASE: Strike the note and bend up as indicated, then release back to the original note. Only the first note is struck.

PRE-BEND: Bend the note as indicated, then strike it.

VIBRATO: The string is vibrated by rapidly bending and releasing the note with the fretting hand.

PALM MUTING: The note is partially muted by the pick hand lightly touching the string(s) just before the bridge.

HAMMER-ON: Strike the first (lower) note with one finger, then sound the higher note (on the same string) with another finger by fretting it without picking.

PULL-OFF: Place both fingers on the notes to be sounded. Strike the first note and without picking, pull the finger off to sound the second (lower) note.

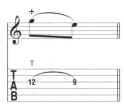

LEGATO SLIDE: Strike the first note and then slide the same fret-hand finger up or down to the second note. The second note is not struck.

SHIFT SLIDE: Same as legato slide, except the second note is struck.

TRILL: Very rapidly alternate between the notes indicated by continuously hammering on and pulling off.

TAPPING: Hammer ("tap") the fret indicated with the pick-hand index or middle finger and pull off to the note fretted by the fret hand.

NATURAL HARMONIC: Strike the note while the fret-hand lightly touches the string directly over the fret indicated.

PINCH HARMONIC: The note is fretted normally and a harmonic is produced by adding the edge of the thumb or the tip of the index finger of the pick hand to the normal pick attack.

TREMOLO PICKING: The note is picked as rapidly and continuously as possible.

VIBRATO BAR DIVE AND RETURN: The pitch of the note or chord is dropped a specified number of steps (in rhythm), then returned to the original pitch.

VIBRATO BAR SCOOP: Depress the bar just before striking the note, then quickly release the bar.

VIBRATO BAR DIP: Strike the note and then immediately drop a specified number of steps, then release back to the original pitch.

Additional Musical Definitions

 (accent) · Accentuate note (play it louder).

 (staccato) · Play the note short.

D.S. al Coda · Go back to the sign (%), then play until the measure marked "**To Coda**," then skip to the section labelled "**Coda**."

D.C. al Fine · Go back to the beginning of the song and play until the measure marked "***Fine***" (end).

Fill · Label used to identify a brief melodic figure which is to be inserted into the arrangement.

N.C. · Harmony is implied.

 · Repeat measures between signs.

· When a repeated section has different endings, play the first ending only the first time and the second ending only the second time.

CONTENTS

All of Me

Words and Music by Seymour Simons and Gerald Marks

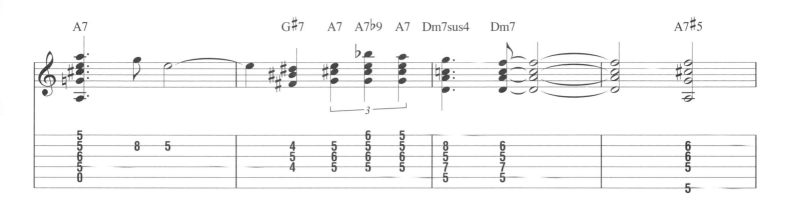

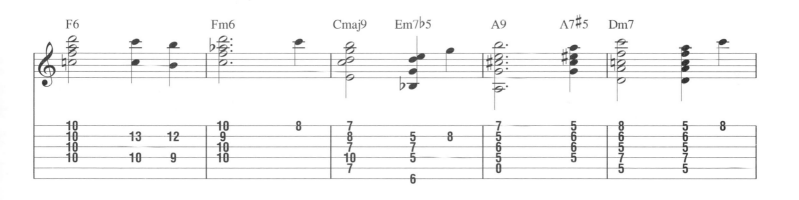

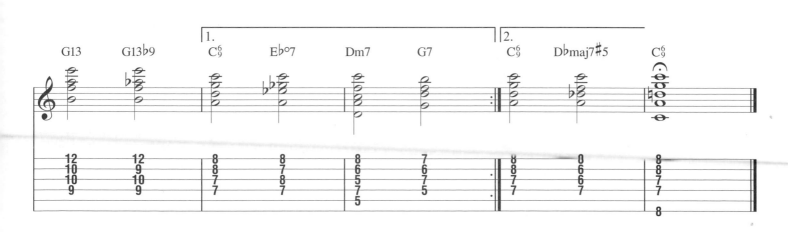

All the Things You Are

from VERY WARM FOR MAY

Lyrics by Oscar Hammerstein II
Music by Jerome Kern

Alone Together

Lyrics by Howard Dietz
Music by Arthur Schwartz

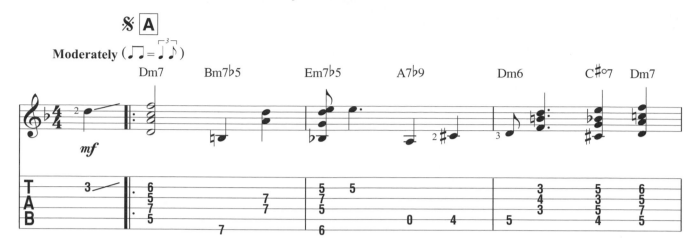

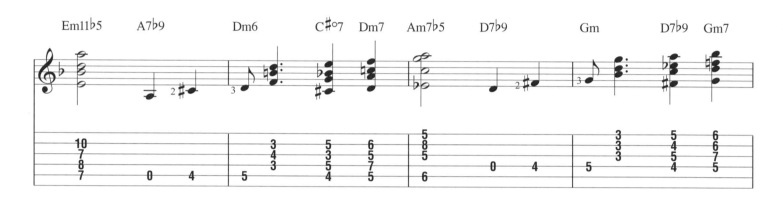

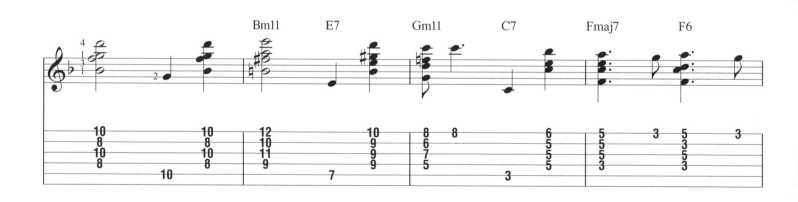

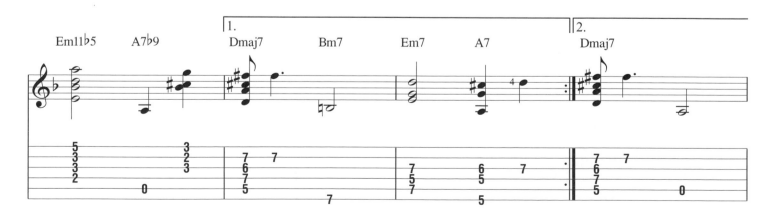

*T = Thumb on 6th string

Autumn in New York

Words and Music by Vernon Duke

Autumn Leaves

English lyric by Johnny Mercer
French lyric by Jacques Prevert
Music by Joseph Kosma

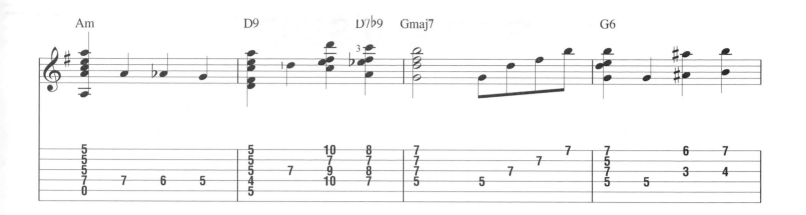

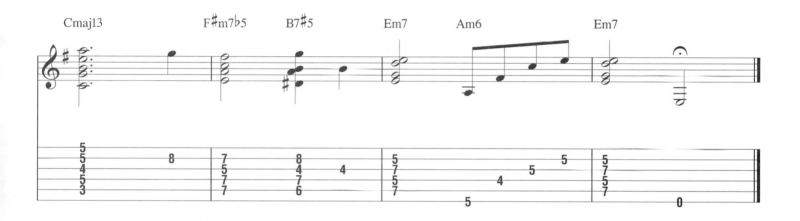

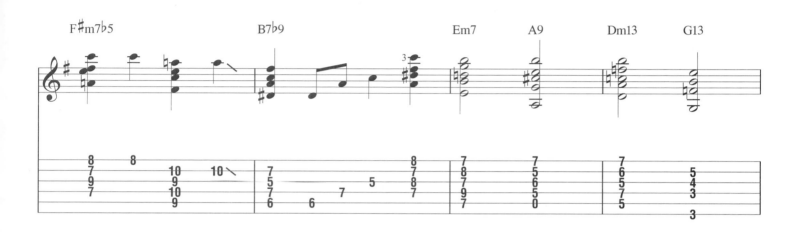

Body and Soul

from THREE'S A CROWD

Words by Edward Heyman, Robert Sour and Frank Eyton
Music by John Green

Easy Living

Theme from the Paramount Picture EASY LIVING

Words and Music by Leo Robin and Ralph Rainger

15

But Not for Me

from GIRL CRAZY

Music and Lyrics by George Gershwin and Ira Gershwin

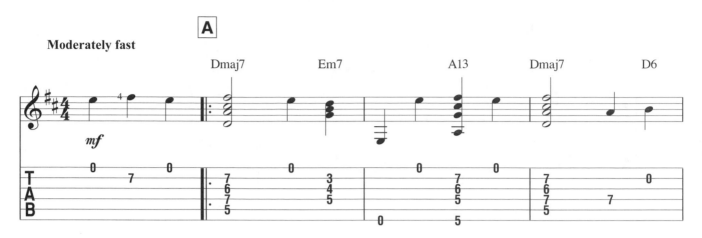

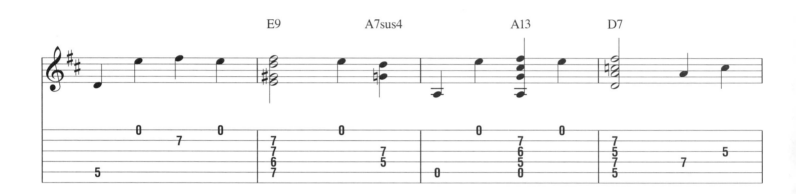

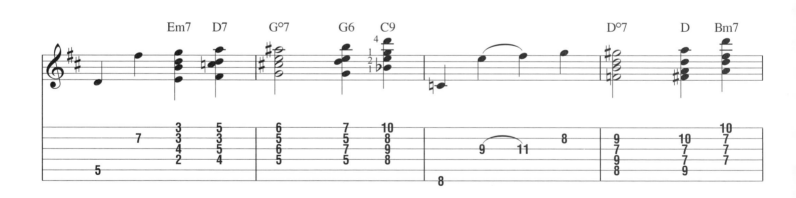

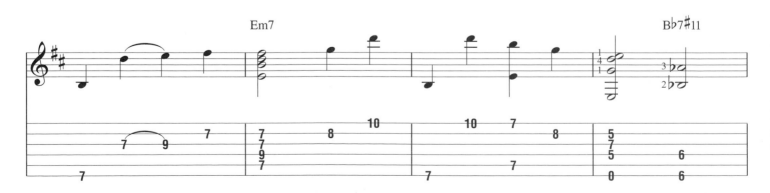

Days of Wine and Roses

from DAYS OF WINE AND ROSES

Lyrics by Johnny Mercer
Music by Henry Mancini

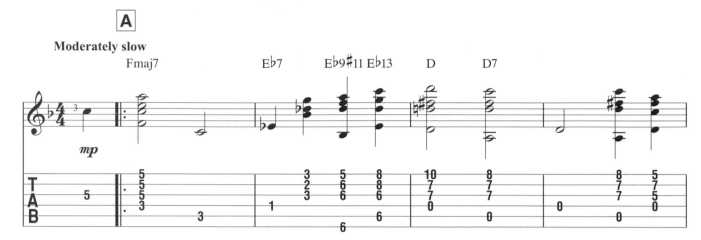

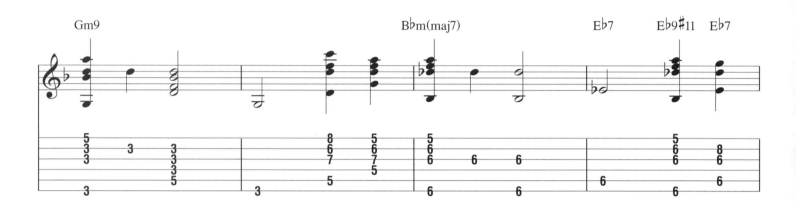

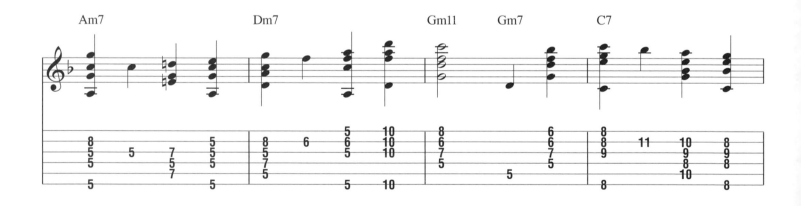

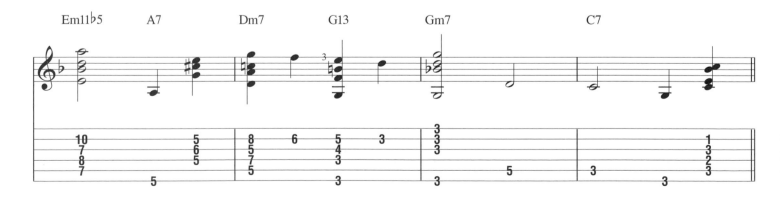

Don't Get Around Much Anymore

Words and Music by Duke Ellington and Bob Russell

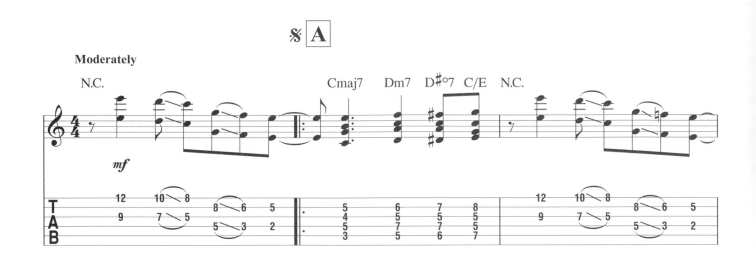

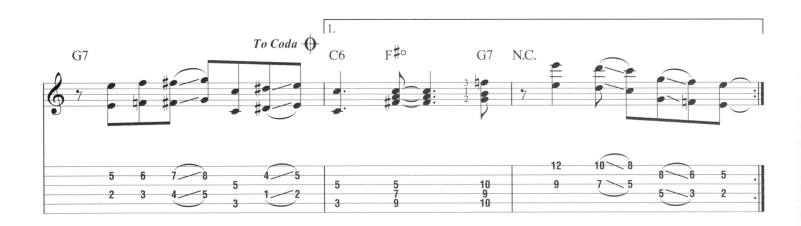

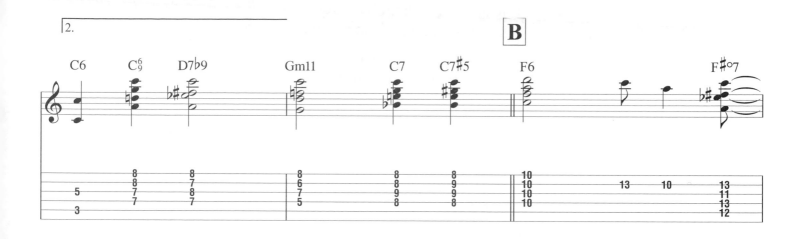

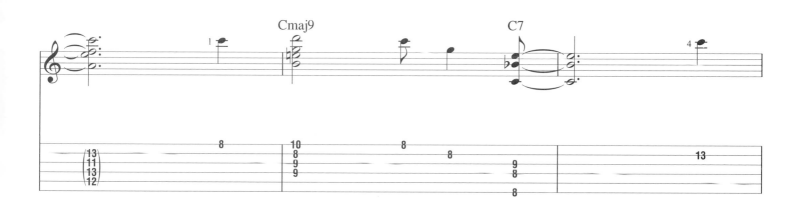

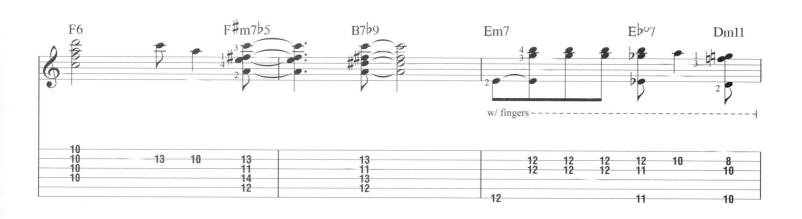

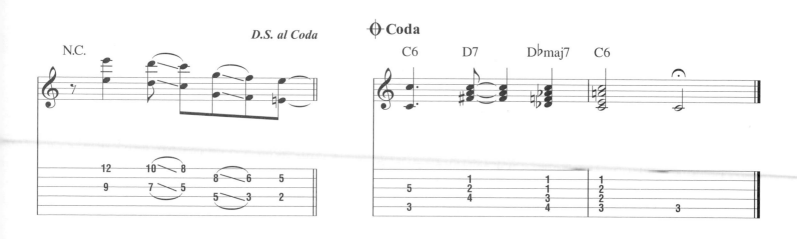

Fly Me to the Moon
(In Other Words)

Words and Music by Bart Howard

A Foggy Day (In London Town)

from A DAMSEL IN DISTRESS

Music and Lyrics by George Gershwin and Ira Gershwin

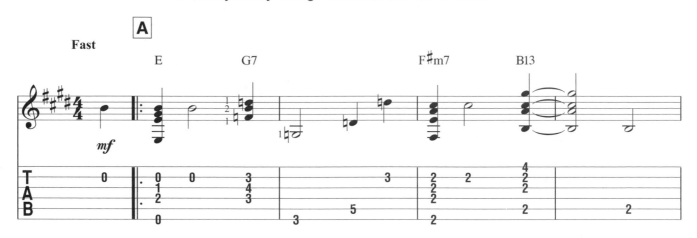

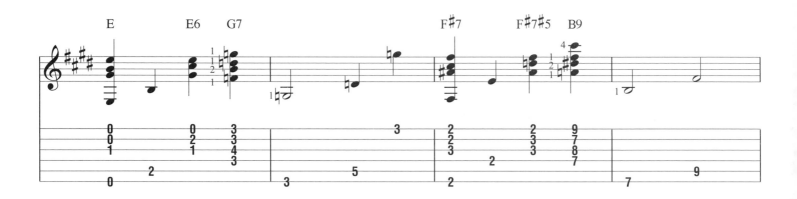

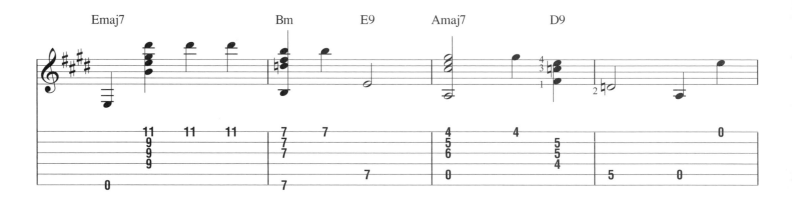

Georgia on My Mind

Words by Stuart Gorrell
Music by Hoagy Carmichael

How High the Moon

from TWO FOR THE SHOW

Lyrics by Nancy Hamilton
Music by Morgan Lewis

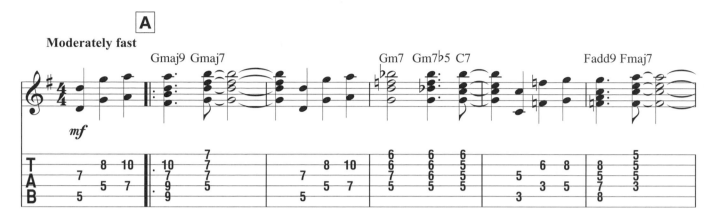

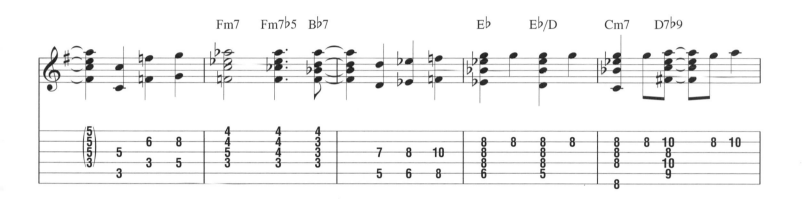

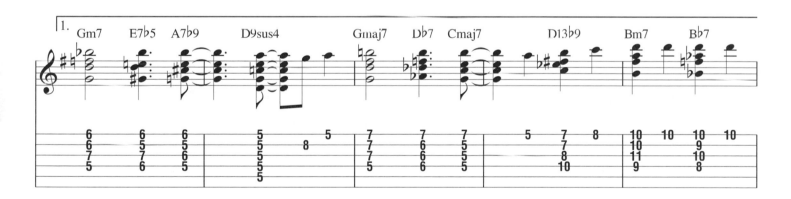

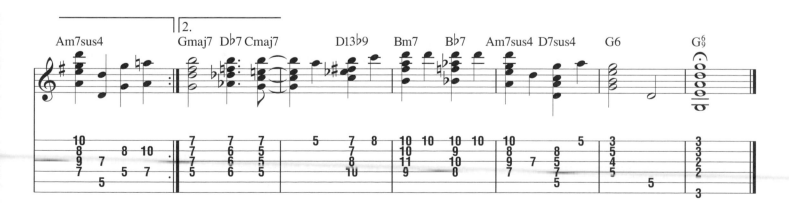

The Girl from Ipanema
(Garôta de Ipanema)

Music by Antonio Carlos Jobim
English Words by Norman Gimbel
Original Words by Vinicius de Moraes

I Can't Get Started

from ZIEGFELD FOLLIES

Words by Ira Gershwin
Music by Vernon Duke

I Got Rhythm

from AN AMERICAN IN PARIS

Music and Lyrics by George Gershwin and Ira Gershwin

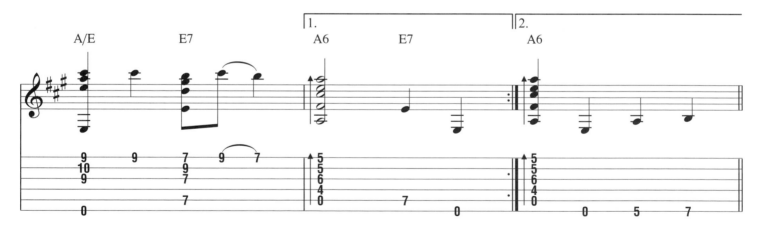

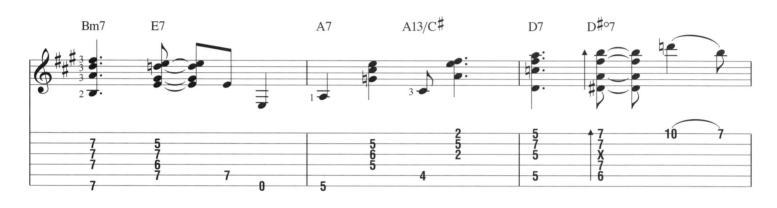

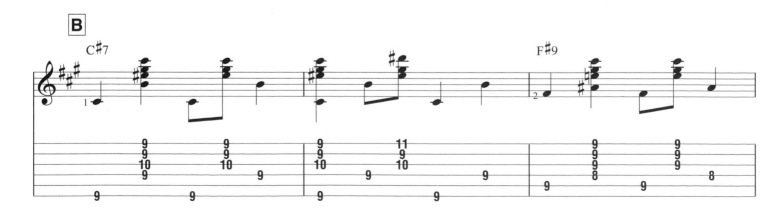

I'll Remember April

Words and Music by Pat Johnson, Don Raye and Gene De Paul

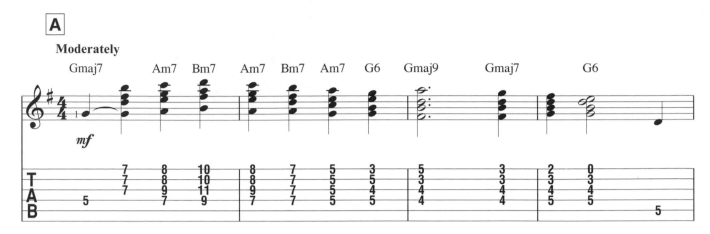

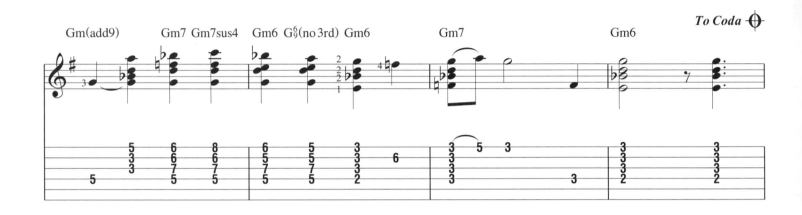

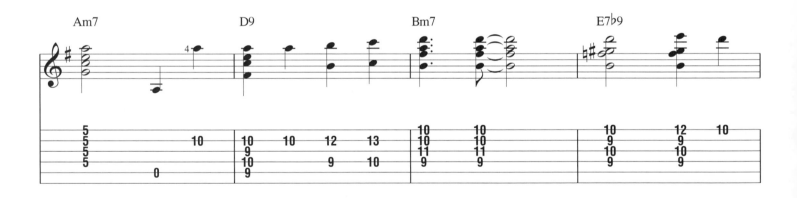

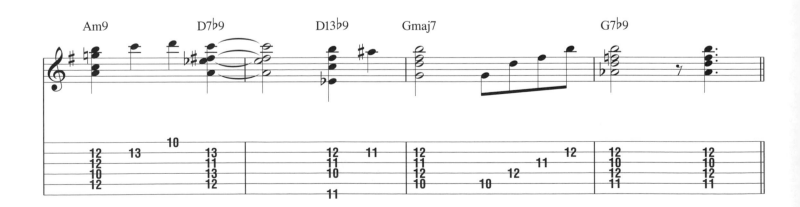

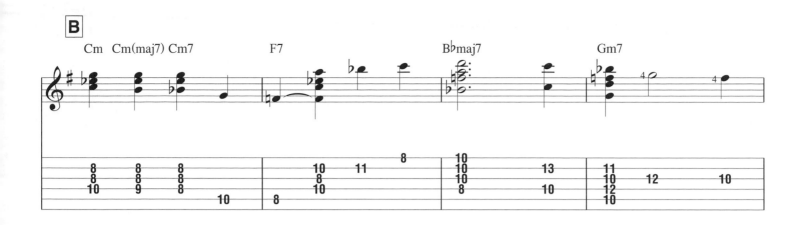

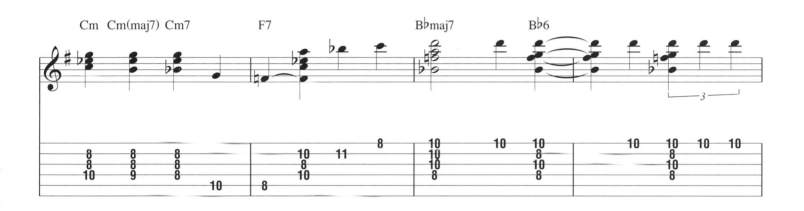

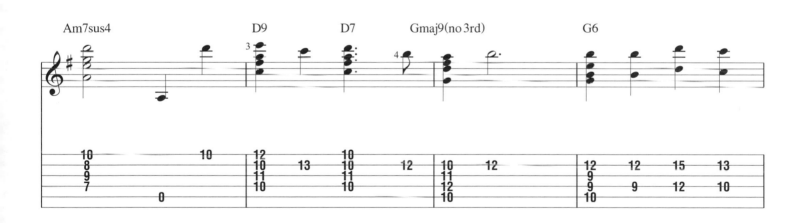

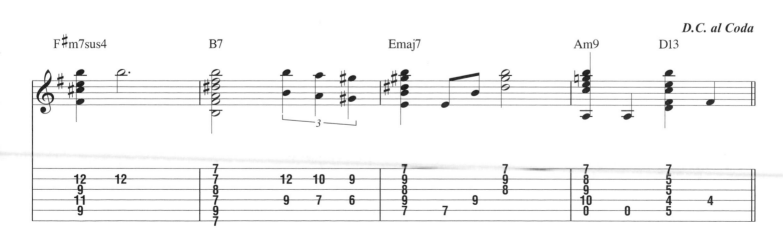

⊕ Coda

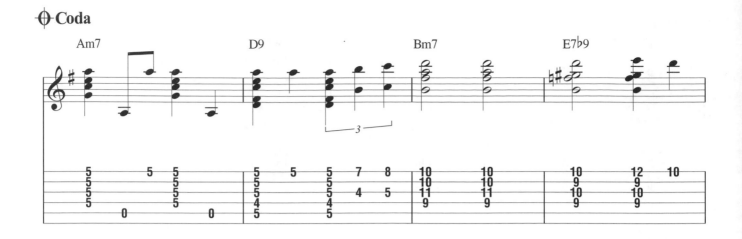

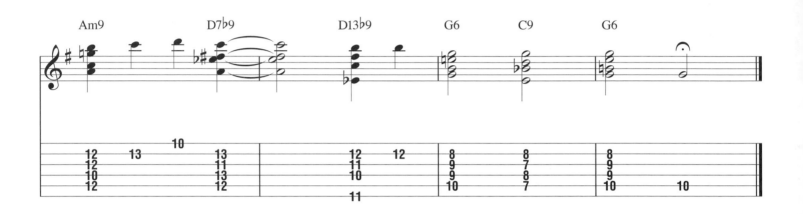

In a Sentimental Mood

Words and Music by Duke Ellington, Irving Mills and Manny Kurtz

If I Should Lose You

from the Paramount Picture ROSE OF THE RANCHO

Words and Music by Leo Robin and Ralph Rainger

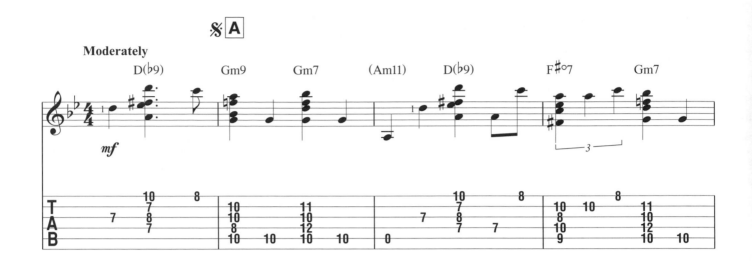

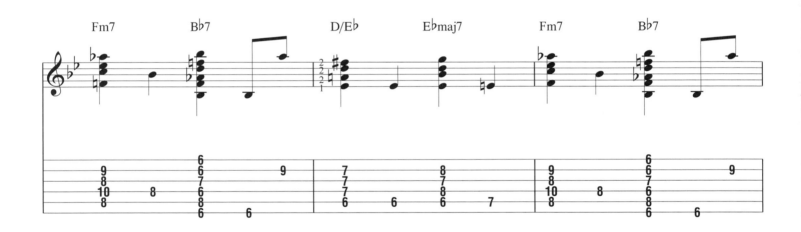

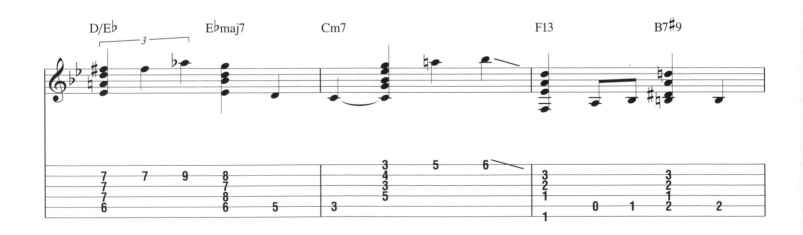

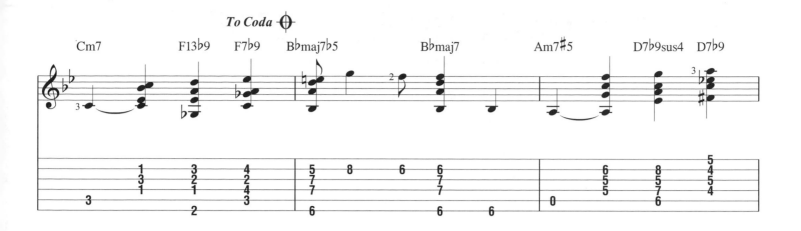

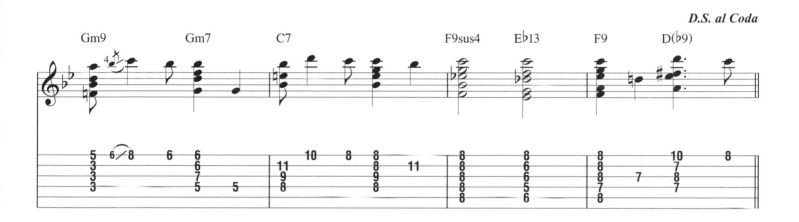

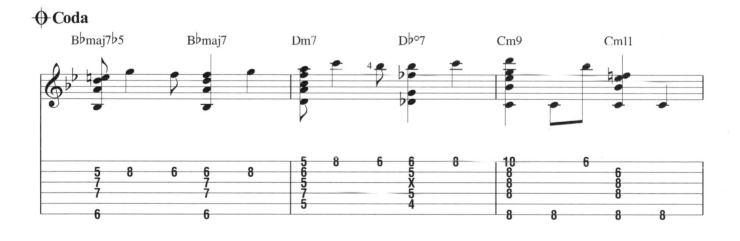

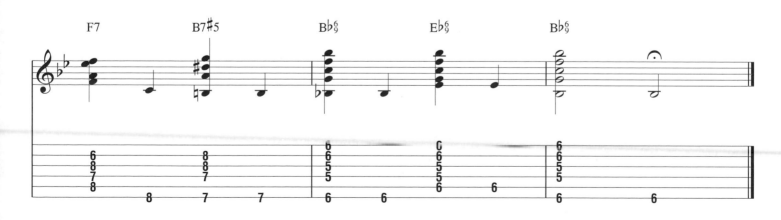

It Could Happen to You

from the Paramount Picture AND THE ANGELS SING
Words by Johnny Burke
Music by James Van Heusen

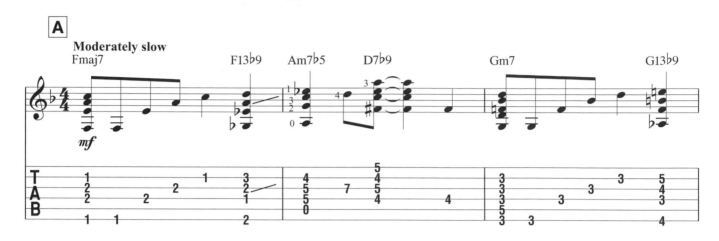

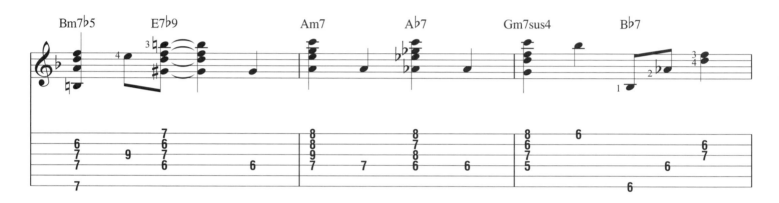

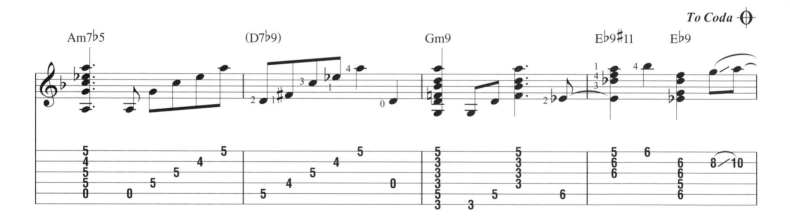

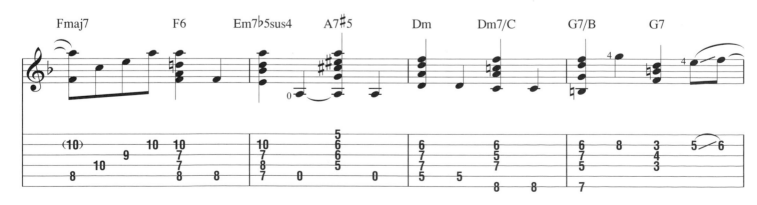

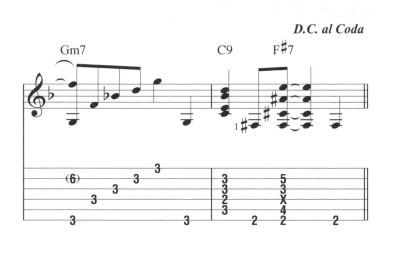

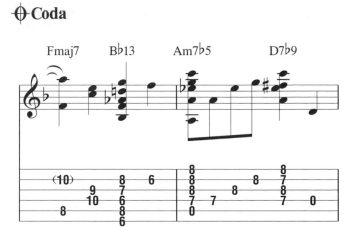

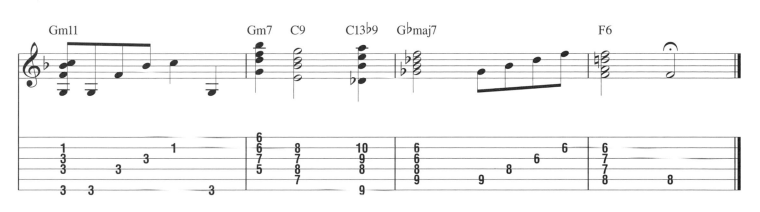

Just Friends

Lyrics by Sam M. Lewis
Music by John Klenner

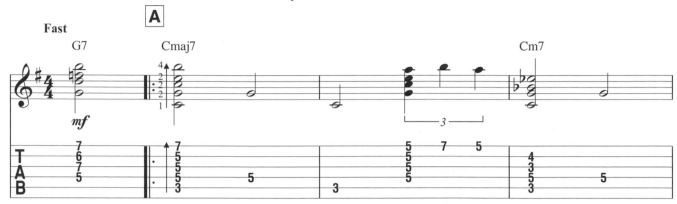

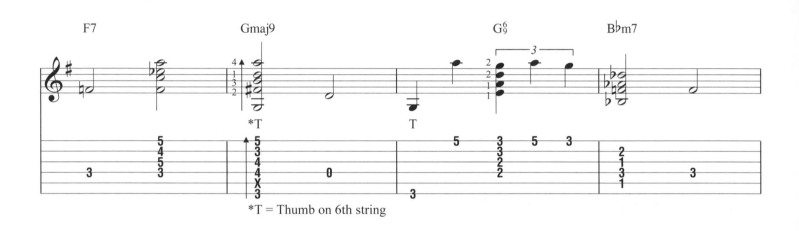

*T = Thumb on 6th string

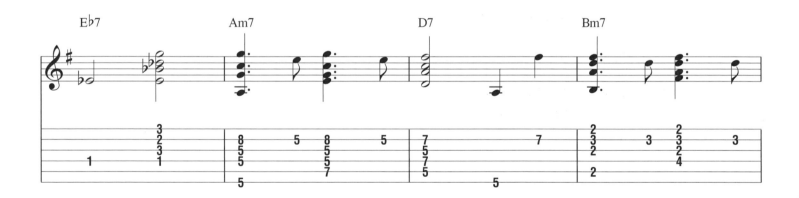

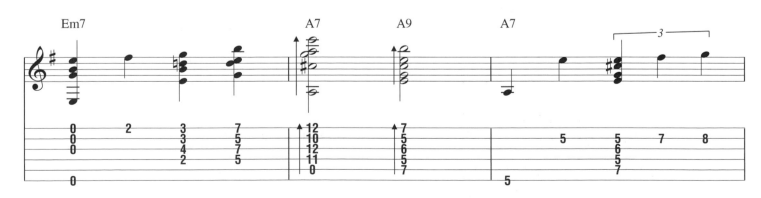

Laura

Lyrics by Johnny Mercer
Music by David Raksin

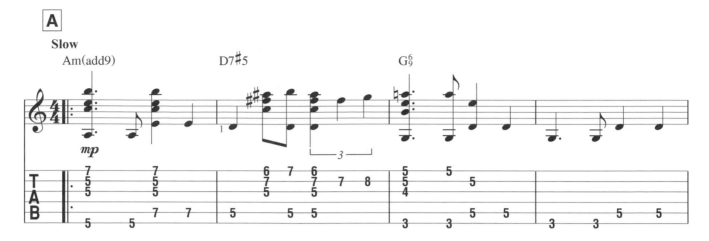

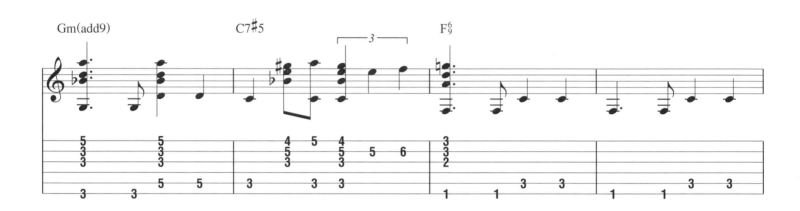

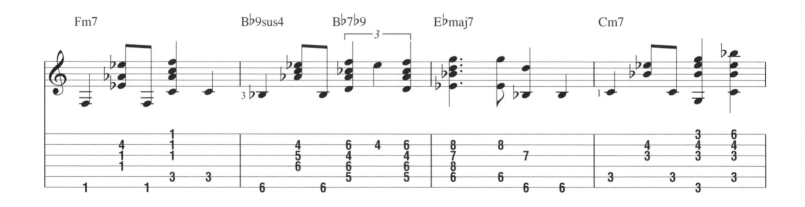

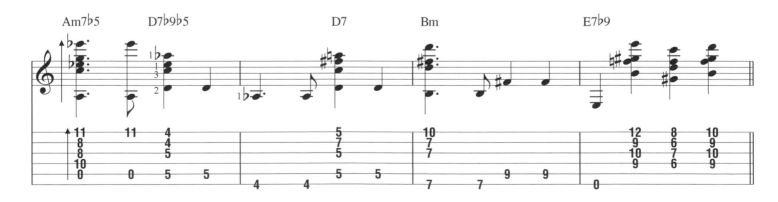

Lover Man
(Oh, Where Can You Be?)
Words and Music by Jimmy Davis, Roger Ramirez and Jimmy Sherman

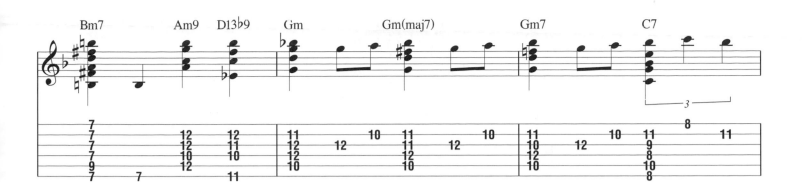

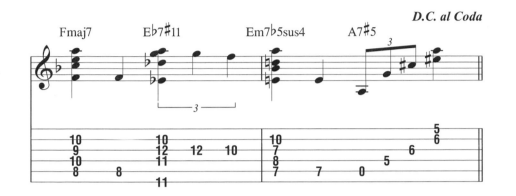

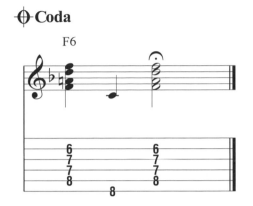

Misty

Words by Johnny Burke
Music by Erroll Garner

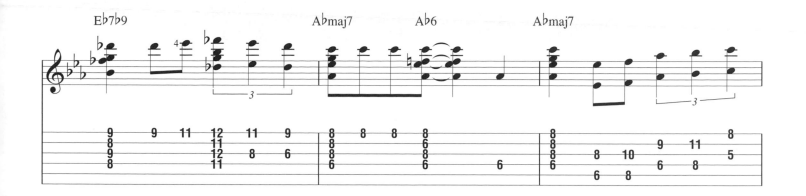

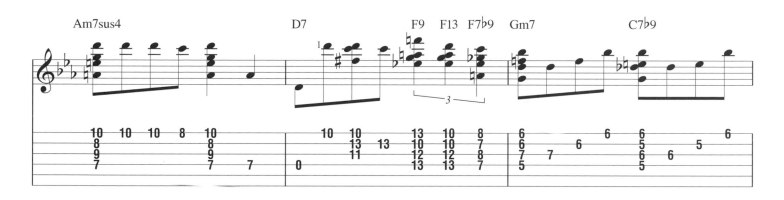

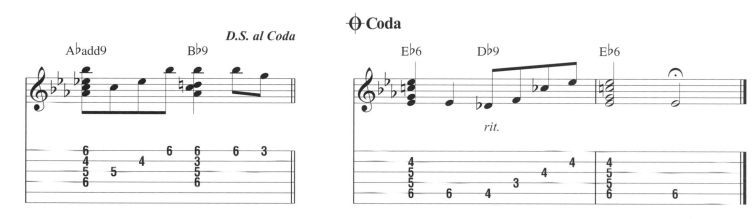

Moonlight in Vermont

Words by John Blackburn
Music by Karl Suessdorf

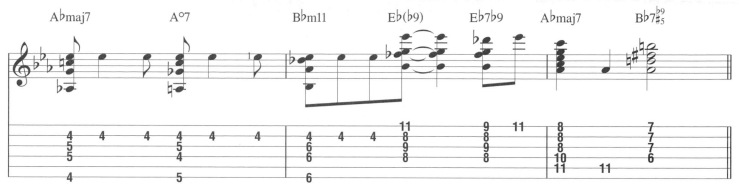

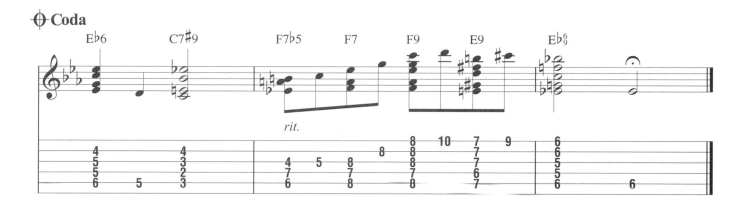

My Funny Valentine

from BABES IN ARMS

Words by Lorenz Hart
Music by Richard Rodgers

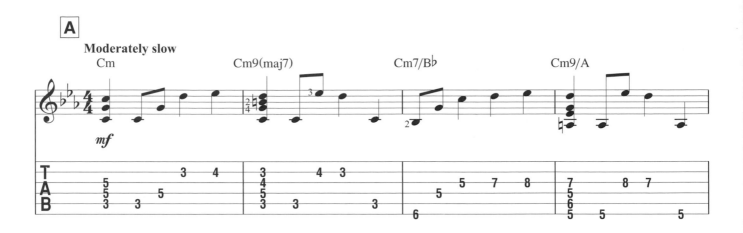

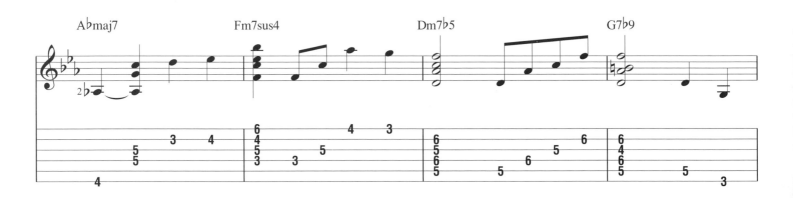

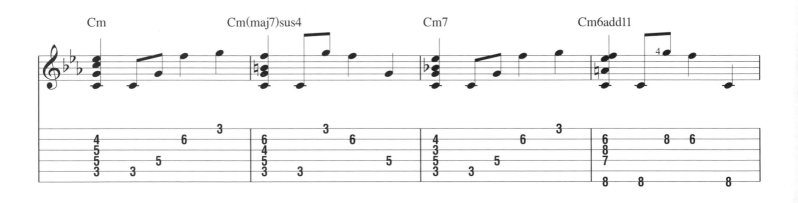

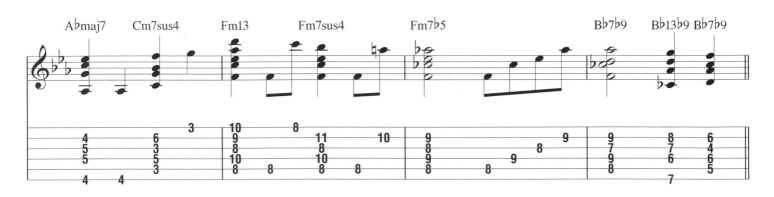

My One and Only Love

Words by Robert Mellin
Music by Guy Wood

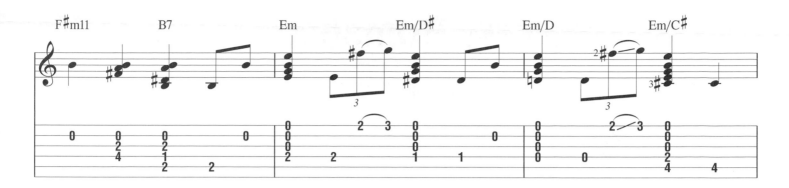

⊕ Coda

D.C. al Coda

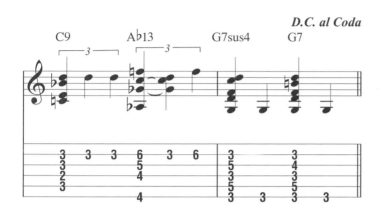

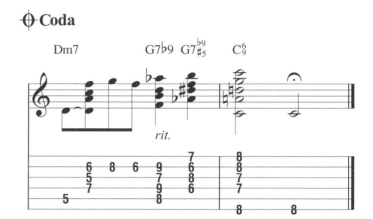

My Romance

from JUMBO

Words by Lorenz Hart
Music by Richard Rodgers

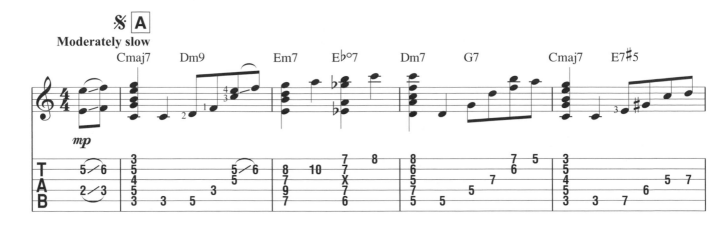

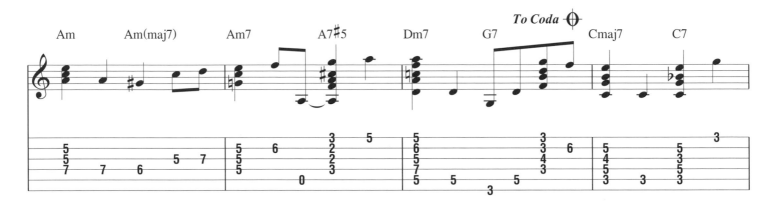

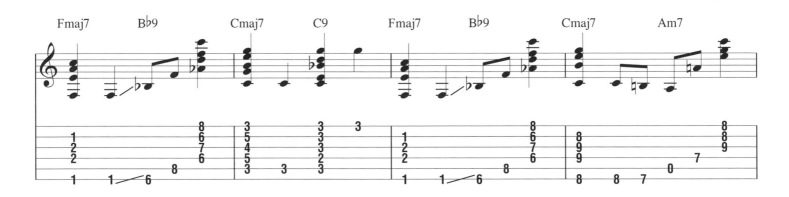

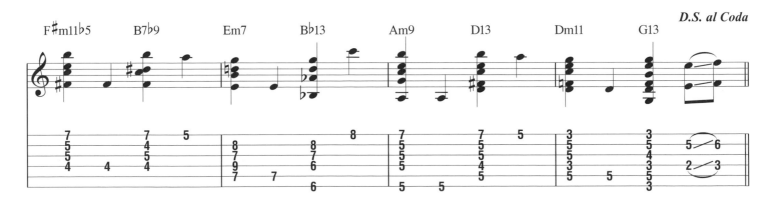

⊕ Coda

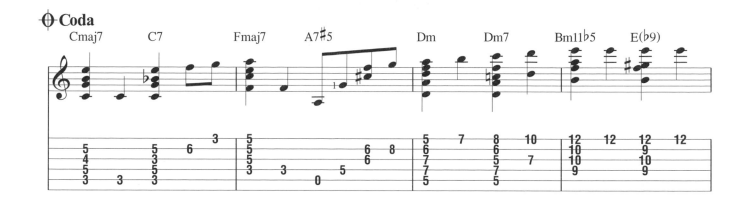

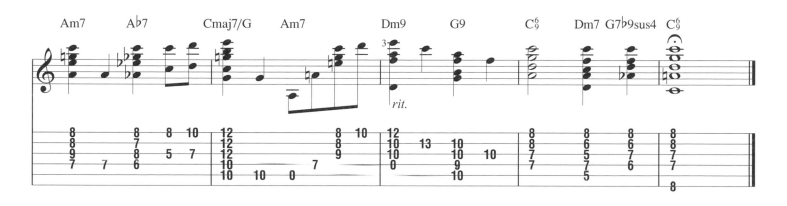

The Nearness of You

from the Paramount Picture ROMANCE IN THE DARK

Words by Ned Washington
Music by Hoagy Carmichael

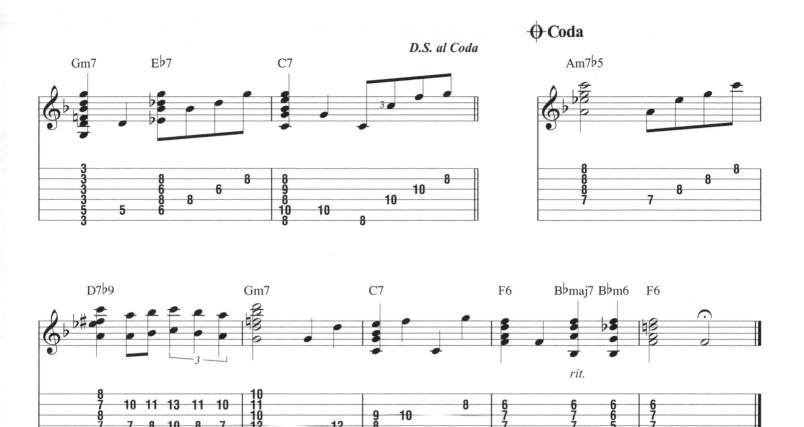

Night and Day

from GAY DIVORCE

Words and Music by Cole Porter

*T = Thumb on 6th string

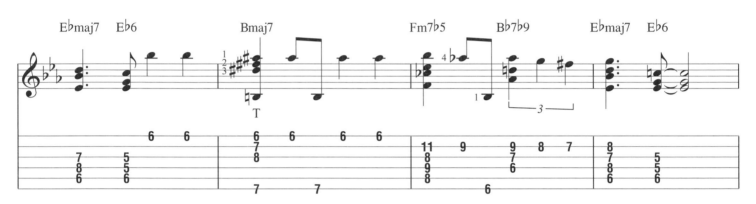

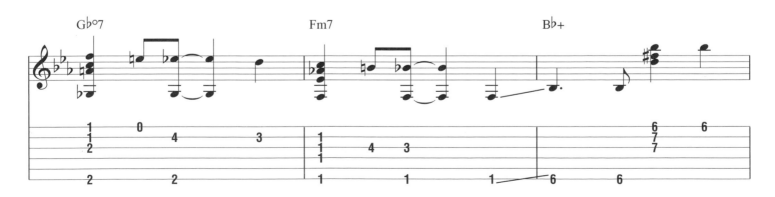

Out of Nowhere

from the Paramount Picture DUDE RANCH

Words by Edward Heyman
Music by Johnny Green

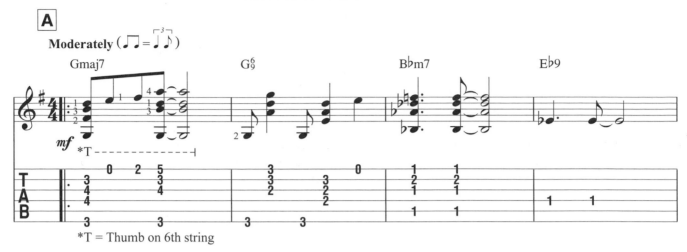

*T = Thumb on 6th string

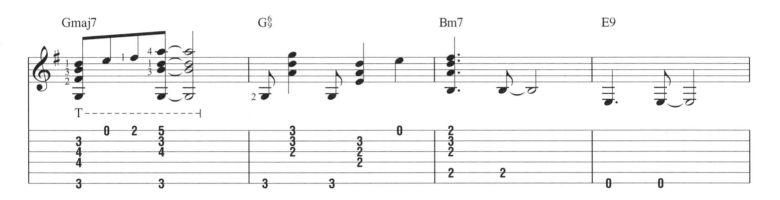

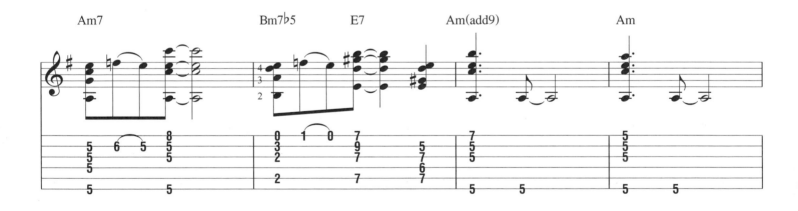

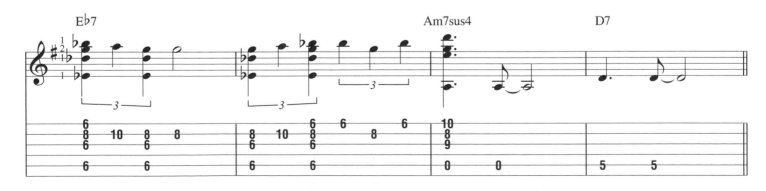

'Round Midnight

Music by Thelonious Monk and Cootie Williams
Words by Bernie Hanighen

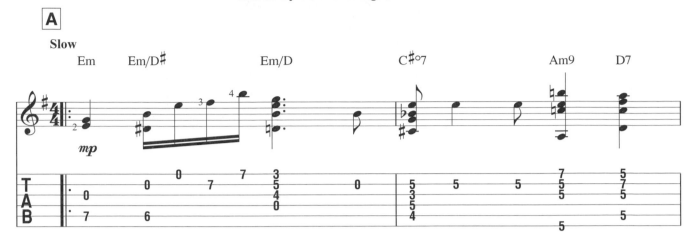

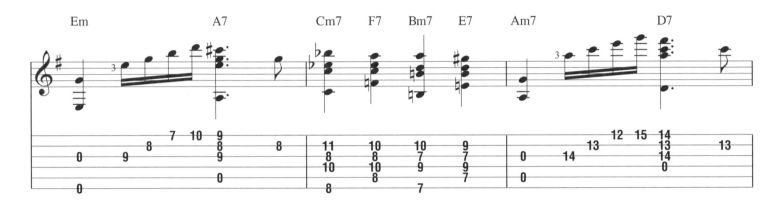

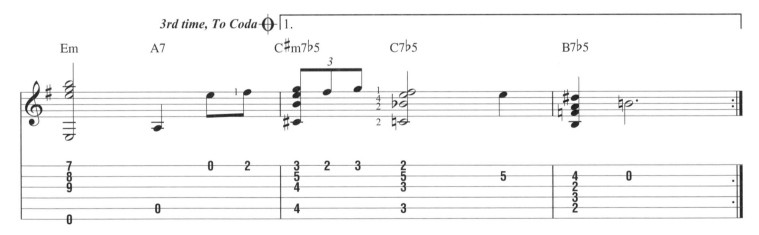

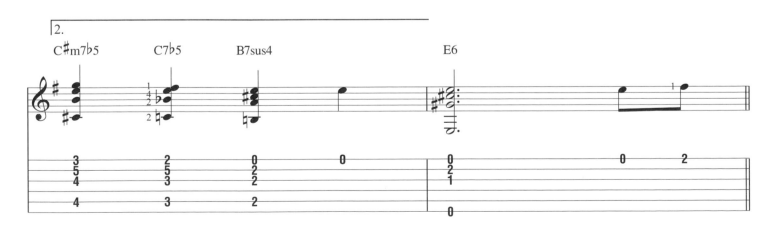

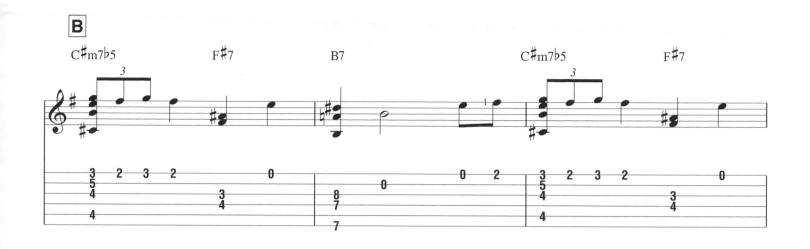

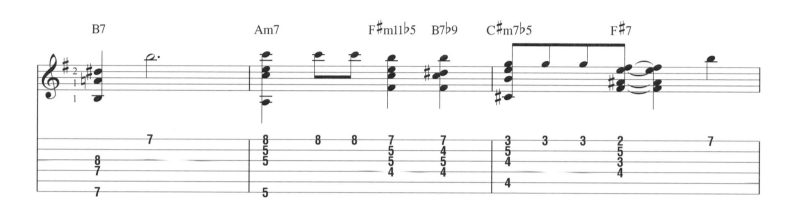

D.C. al Coda

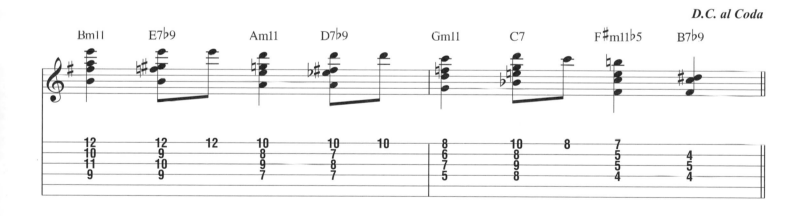

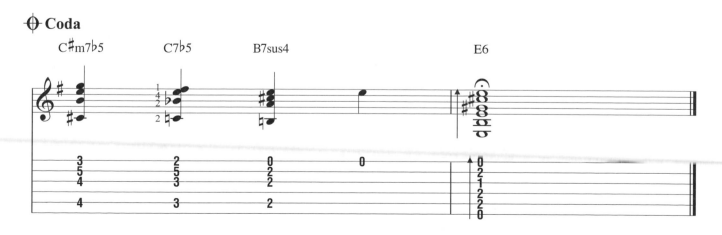

Satin Doll

from SOPHISTICATED LADIES

Words by Johnny Mercer and Billy Strayhorn
Music by Duke Ellington

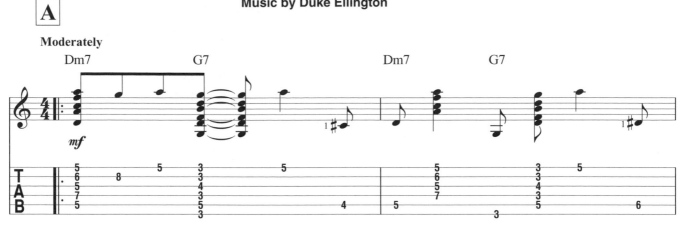

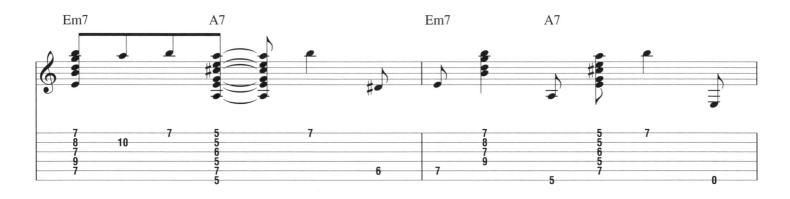

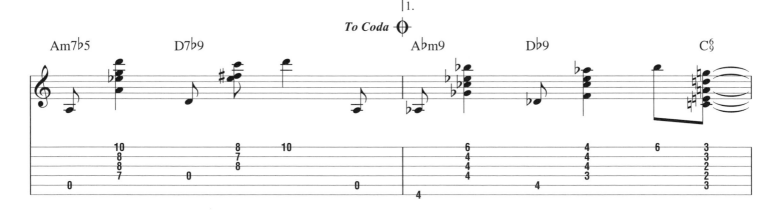

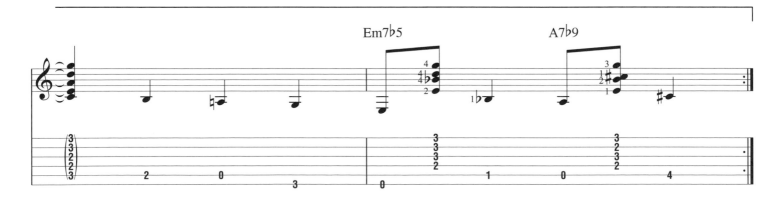

Softly as in a Morning Sunrise

from THE NEW MOON

Lyrics by Oscar Hammerstein II
Music by Sigmund Romberg

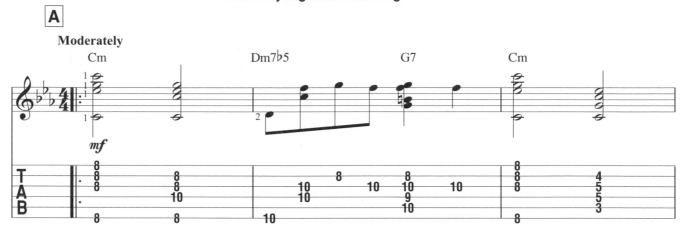

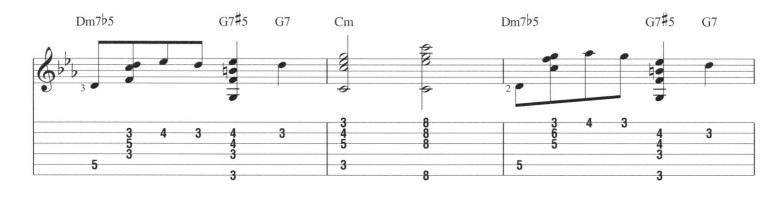

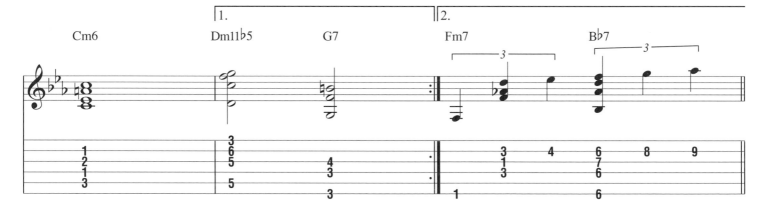

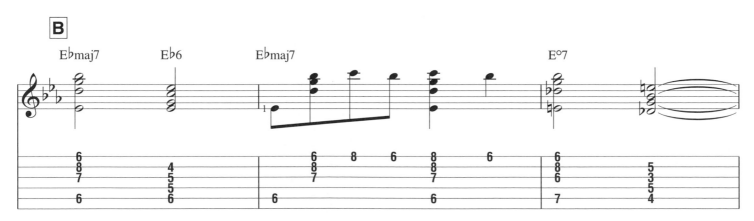

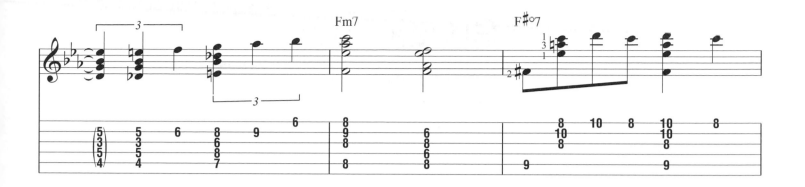

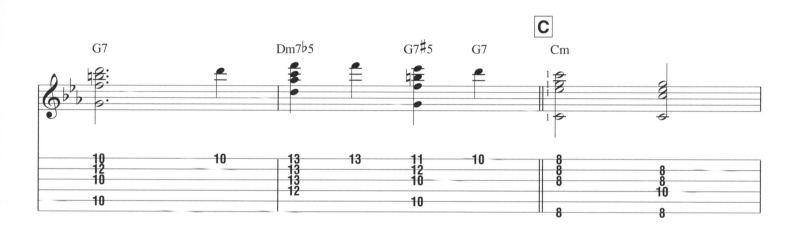

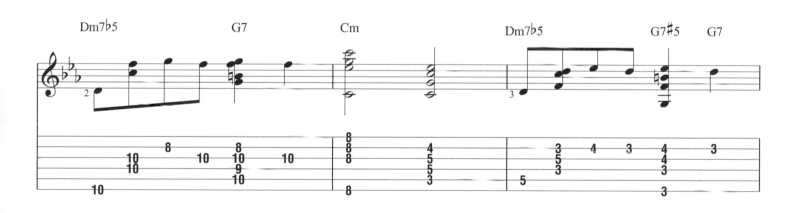

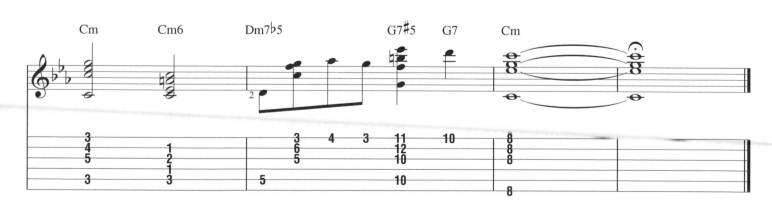

Speak Low

from the Musical Production ONE TOUCH OF VENUS
Words by Ogden Nash
Music by Kurt Weill

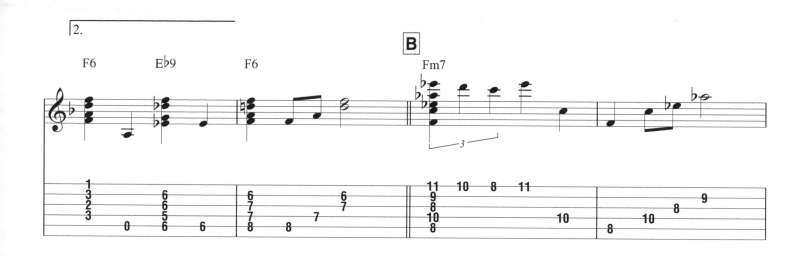

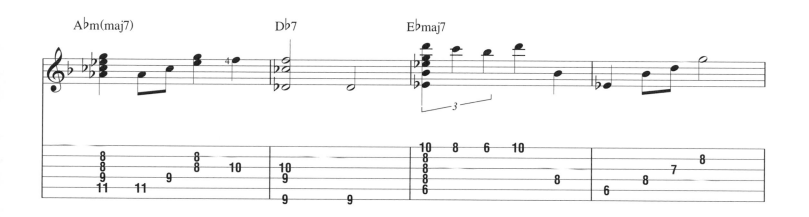

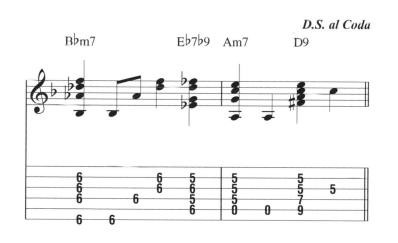
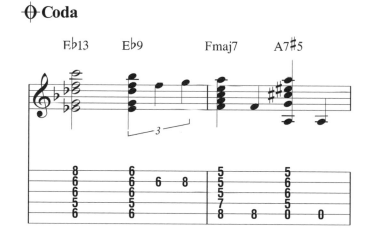

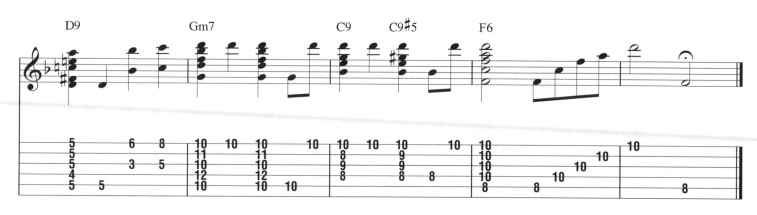

Star Eyes

Words by Don Raye
Music by Gene De Paul

73

Stardust

Words by Mitchell Parish
Music by Hoagy Carmichael

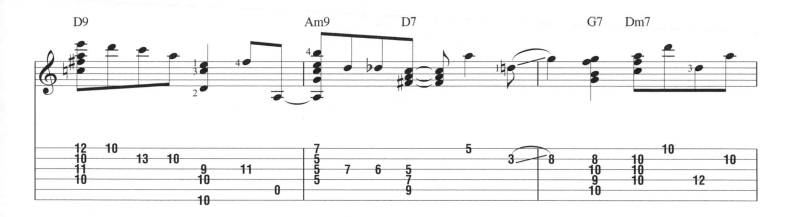

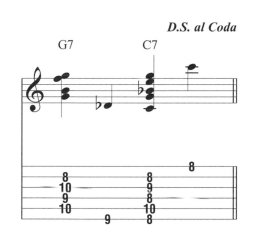

⊕ Coda

D.S. al Coda

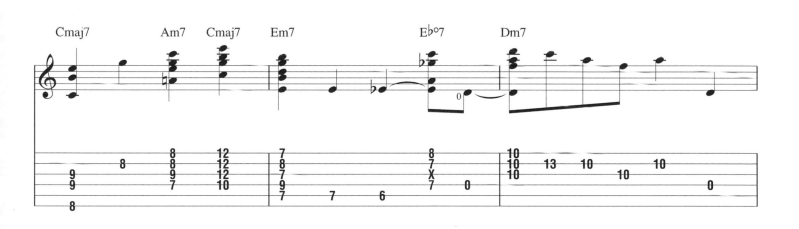

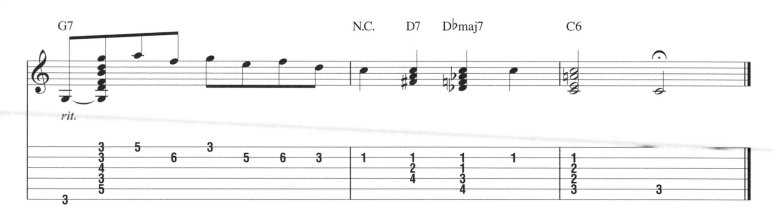

Stella by Starlight

from the Paramount Picture THE UNINVITED

Words by Ned Washington
Music by Victor Young

A

Moderately slow

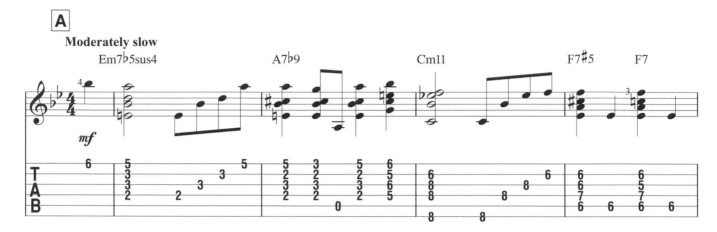

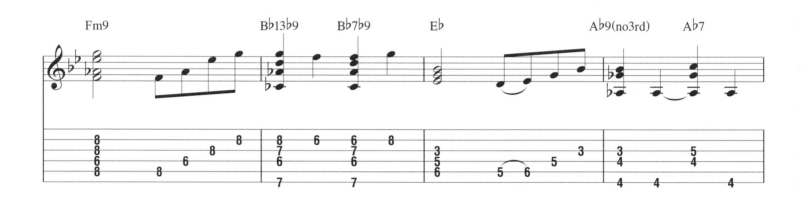

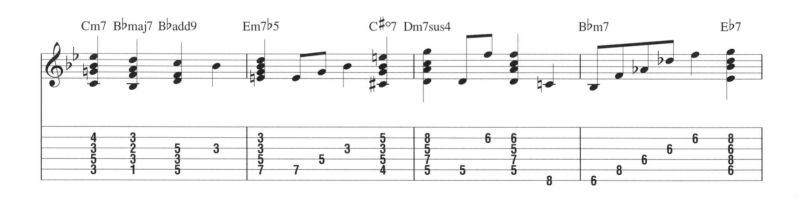

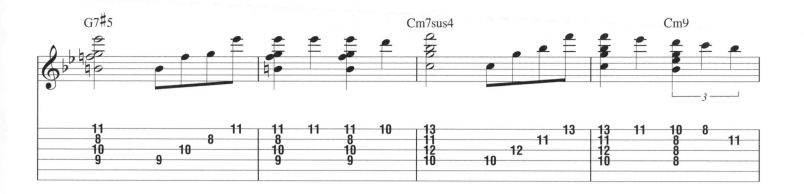

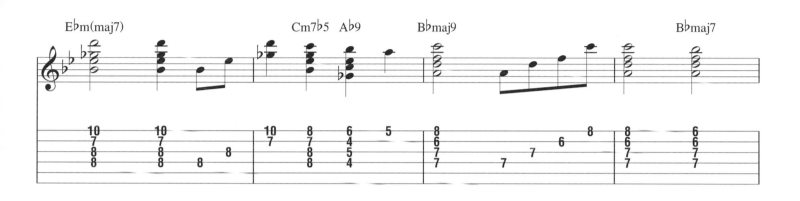

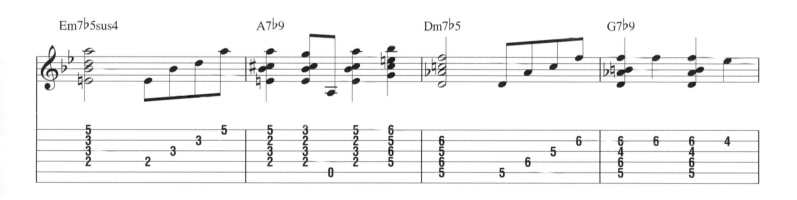

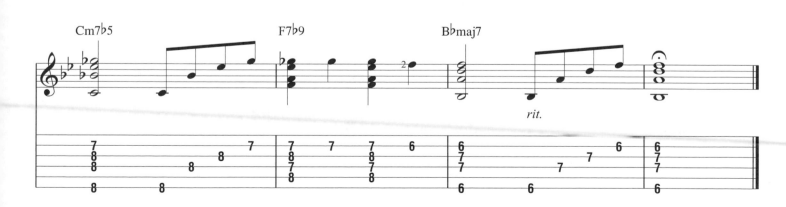

Summertime
from PORGY AND BESS®

Music and Lyrics by George Gershwin, DuBose and Dorothy Heyward and Ira Gershwin

Tangerine

from the Paramount Picture THE FLEET'S IN
Words by Johnny Mercer
Music by Victor Schertzinger

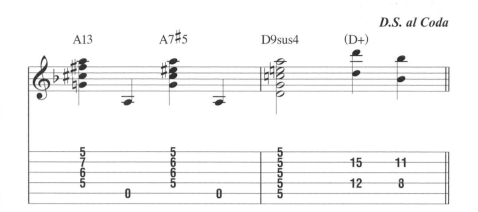

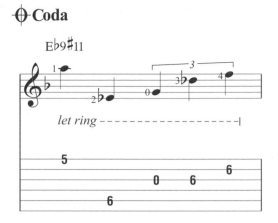

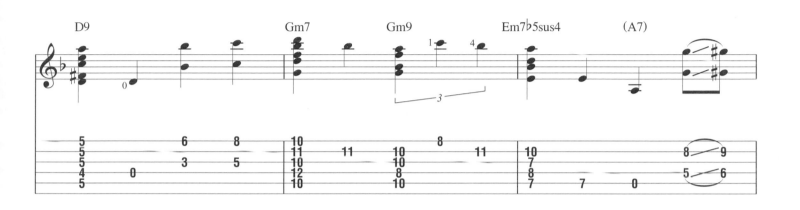

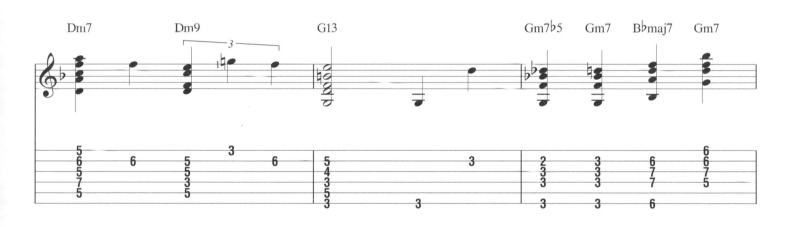

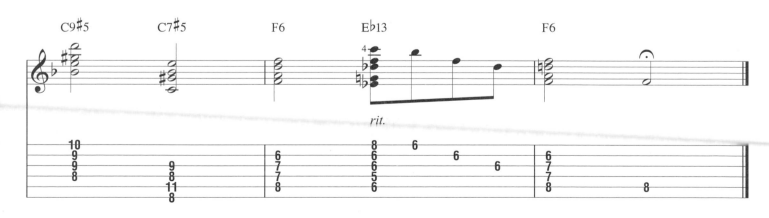

Tenderly

from TORCH SONG

Lyric by Jack Lawrence
Music by Walter Gross

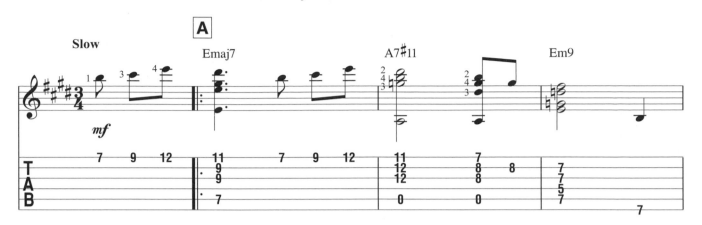

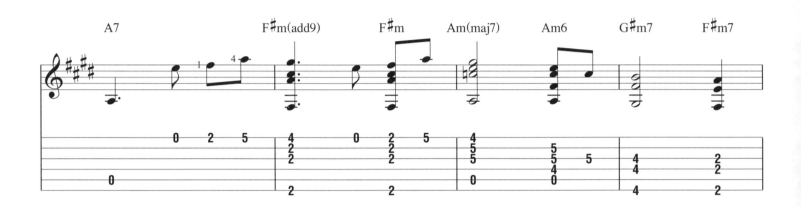

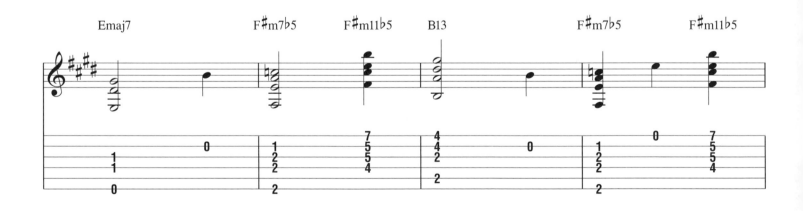

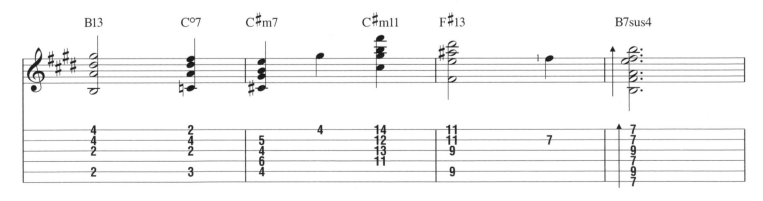

There Is No Greater Love

Words by Marty Symes
Music by Isham Jones

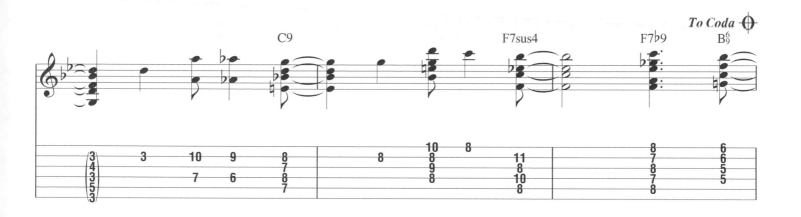

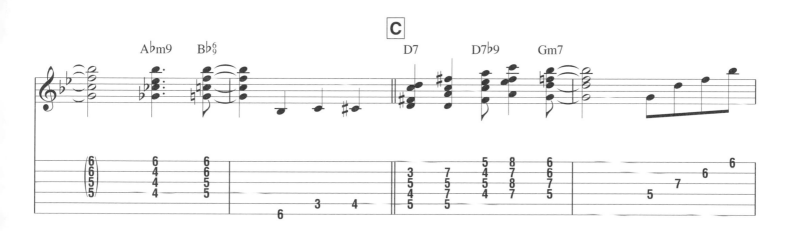

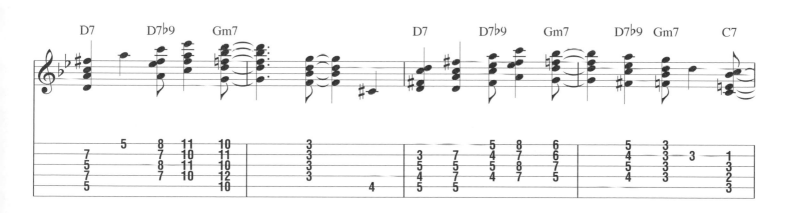

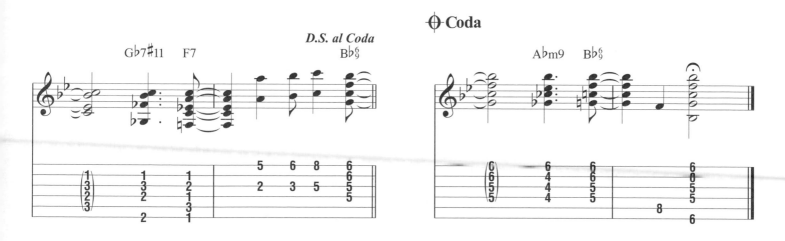

There Will Never Be Another You

from the Motion Picture ICELAND

Lyric by Mack Gordon
Music by Harry Warren

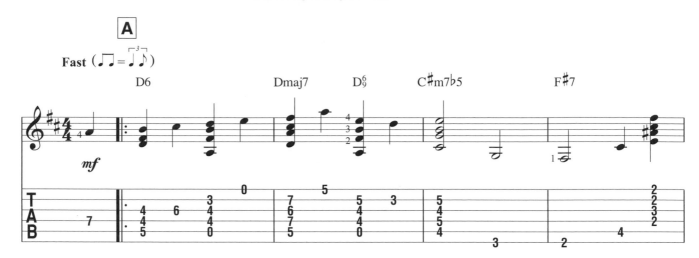

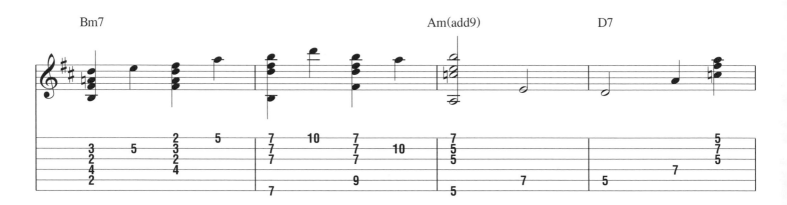

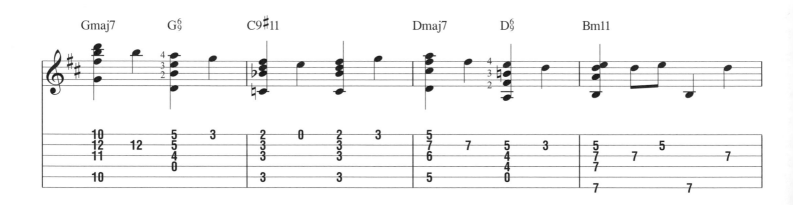

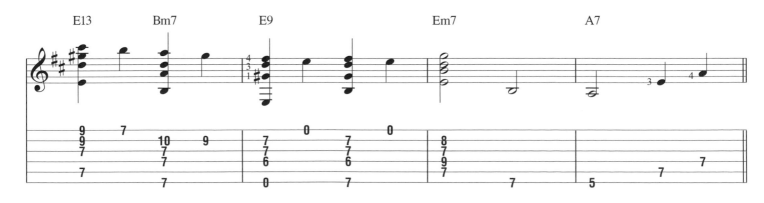

The Way You Look Tonight

from SWING TIME

Words by Dorothy Fields
Music by Jerome Kern

When I Fall in Love

Words by Edward Heyman
Music by Victor Young

Coda

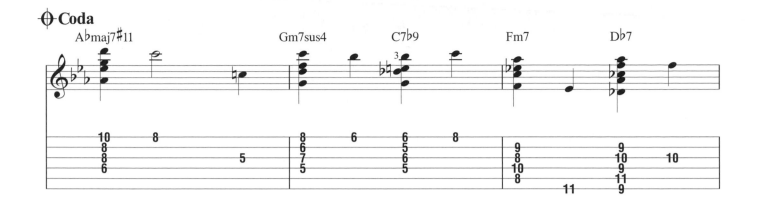

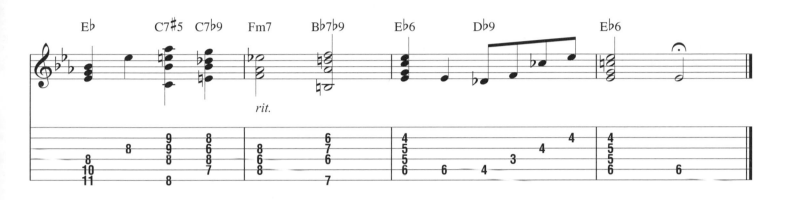

When Sunny Gets Blue

Lyric by Jack Segal
Music by Marvin Fisher

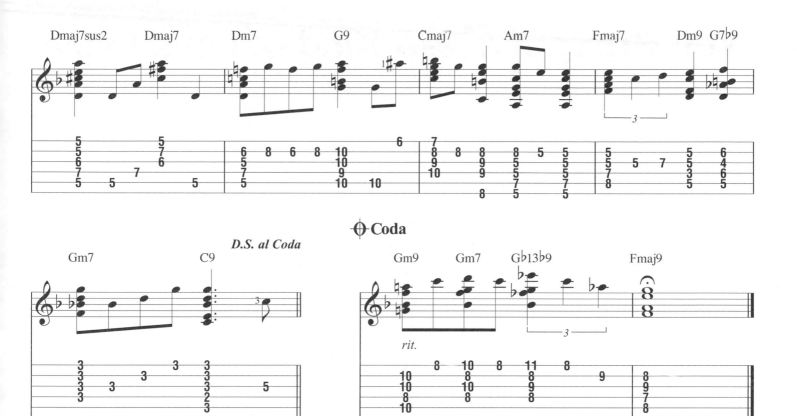

Coda

You Brought a New Kind of Love to Me

from the Paramount Picture THE BIG POND

Words and Music by Sammy Fain, Irving Kahal and Pierre Norman

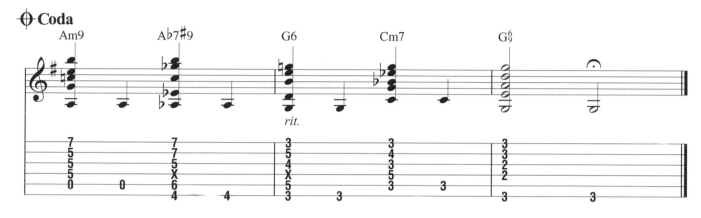

You Stepped Out of a Dream

from the M-G-M Picture ZIEGFELD GIRL

Words by Gus Kahn
Music by Nacio Herb Brown

A

Moderately

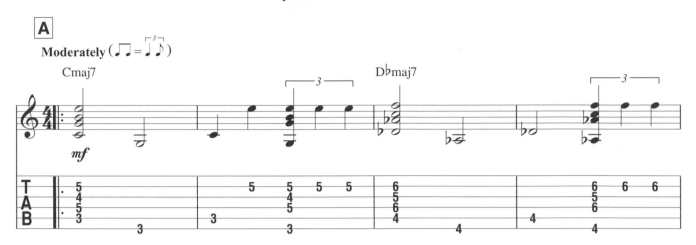

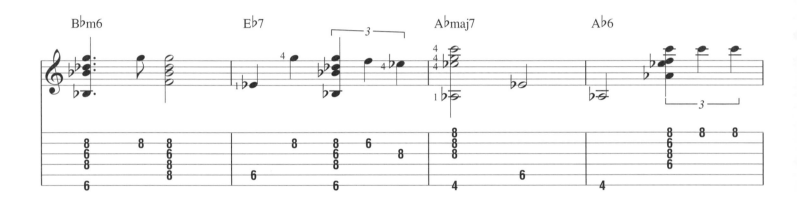

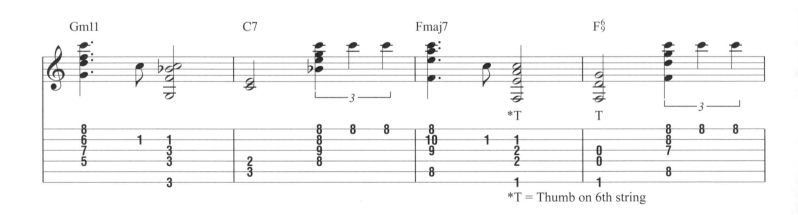

*T = Thumb on 6th string

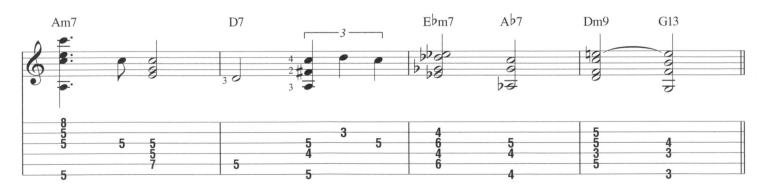

The Song Is You

from MUSIC IN THE AIR

Lyrics by Oscar Hammerstein II
Music by Jerome Kern

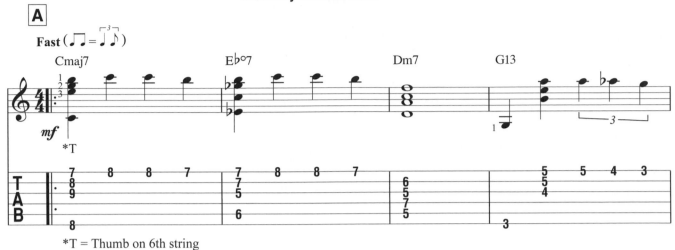

*T = Thumb on 6th string

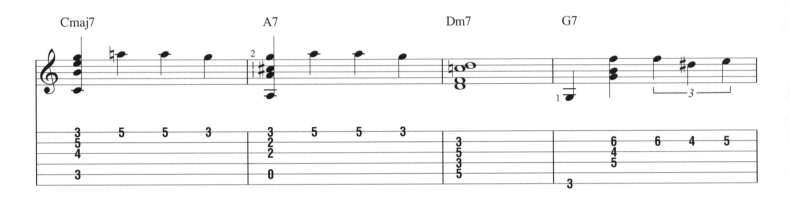

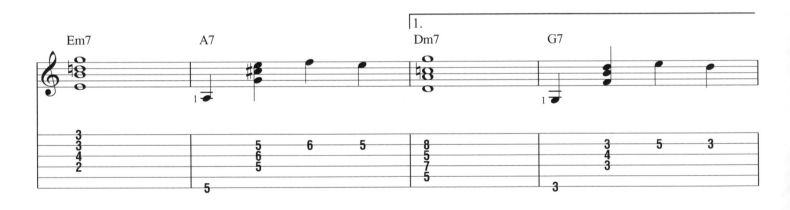

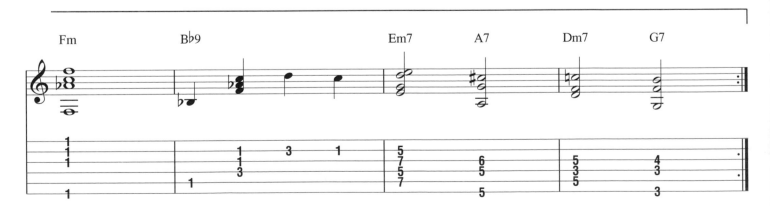

JAZZ GUITAR CHORD MELODY SOLOS

This series features chord melody arrangements in standard notation and tablature of songs for intermediate guitarists.

ALL-TIME STANDARDS

27 songs, including: All of Me • Bewitched • Come Fly with Me • A Fine Romance • Georgia on My Mind • How High the Moon • I'll Never Smile Again • I've Got You Under My Skin • It's De-Lovely • It's Only a Paper Moon • My Romance • Satin Doll • The Surrey with the Fringe on Top • Yesterdays • and more.
00699757 Solo Guitar...........................$16.99

IRVING BERLIN

27 songs, including: Alexander's Ragtime Band • Always • Blue Skies • Cheek to Cheek • Easter Parade • Happy Holiday • Heat Wave • How Deep Is the Ocean • Puttin' On the Ritz • Remember • They Say It's Wonderful • What'll I Do? • White Christmas • and more.
00700637 Solo Guitar...........................$14.99

CHRISTMAS CAROLS

26 songs, including: Auld Lang Syne • Away in a Manger • Deck the Hall • God Rest Ye Merry, Gentlemen • Good King Wenceslas • Here We Come A-Wassailing • It Came upon the Midnight Clear • Joy to the World • O Holy Night • O Little Town of Bethlehem • Silent Night • Toyland • We Three Kings of Orient Are • and more.
00701697 Solo Guitar $14.99

CHRISTMAS JAZZ

21 songs, including Auld Lang Syne • Baby, It's Cold Outside • Cool Yule • Have Yourself a Merry Little Christmas • I've Got My Love to Keep Me Warm • Mary, Did You Know? • Santa Baby • Sleigh Ride • White Christmas • Winter Wonderland • and more.
00171334 Solo Guitar $15.99

DISNEY SONGS

27 songs, including: Beauty and the Beast • Can You Feel the Love Tonight • Candle on the Water • Colors of the Wind • A Dream Is a Wish Your Heart Makes • Heigh-Ho • Some Day My Prince Will Come • Under the Sea • When You Wish upon a Star • A Whole New World (Aladdin's Theme) • Zip-A-Dee-Doo-Dah • and more.
00701902 Solo Guitar $14.99

DUKE ELLINGTON

25 songs, including: C-Jam Blues • Caravan • Do Nothin' Till You Hear from Me • Don't Get Around Much Anymore • I Got It Bad and That Ain't Good • I'm Just a Lucky So and So • In a Sentimental Mood • It Don't Mean a Thing (If It Ain't Got That Swing) • Mood Indigo • Perdido • Prelude to a Kiss • Satin Doll • and more.
00700636 Solo Guitar $14.99

FAVORITE STANDARDS

27 songs, including: All the Way • Autumn in New York • Blue Skies • Cheek to Cheek • Don't Get Around Much Anymore • How Deep Is the Ocean • I'll Be Seeing You • Isn't It Romantic? • It Could Happen to You • The Lady Is a Tramp • Moon River • Speak Low • Take the "A" Train • Willow Weep for Me • Witchcraft • and more.
00699756 Solo Guitar...........................$17.99

JAZZ BALLADS

27 songs, including: Body and Soul • Darn That Dream • Easy to Love (You'd Be So Easy to Love) • Here's That Rainy Day • In a Sentimental Mood • Misty • My Foolish Heart • My Funny Valentine • The Nearness of You • Stella by Starlight • Time After Time • The Way You Look Tonight • When Sunny Gets Blue • and more.
00699755 Solo Guitar..........................$16.99

LATIN STANDARDS

27 Latin favorites, including: Água De Beber (Water to Drink) • Desafinado • The Girl from Ipanema • How Insensitive (Insensatez) • Little Boat • Meditation • One Note Samba (Samba De Uma Nota So) • Poinciana • Quiet Nights of Quiet Stars • Samba De Orfeu • So Nice (Summer Samba) • Wave • and more.
00699754 Solo Guitar...........................$16.99

Order online at **halleonard.com**

IMPROVE YOUR IMPROV
AND OTHER JAZZ TECHNIQUES WITH BOOKS FROM HAL LEONARD

JAZZ GUITAR
HAL LEONARD GUITAR METHOD
by Jeff Schroedl

The Hal Leonard Jazz Guitar Method is your complete guide to learning jazz guitar. This book uses real jazz songs to teach the basics of accompanying and improvising jazz guitar in the style of Wes Montgomery, Joe Pass, Tal Farlow, Charlie Christian, Pat Martino, Barney Kessel, Jim Hall, and many others.
00695359 Book/Online Audio $19.99

AMAZING PHRASING
50 WAYS TO IMPROVE YOUR
IMPROVISATIONAL SKILLS • *by Tom Kolb*

This book explores all the main components necessary for crafting well-balanced rhythmic and melodic phrases. It also explains how these phrases are put together to form cohesive solos. Many styles are covered – rock, blues, jazz, fusion, country, Latin, funk and more – and all of the concepts are backed up with musical examples.
00695583 Book/Online Audio $19.99

BEST OF JAZZ GUITAR
by Wolf Marshall • Signature Licks

In this book/CD pack, Wolf Marshall provides a hands-on analysis of 10 of the most frequently played tunes in the jazz genre, as played by the leading guitarists of all time. Each selection includes technical analysis and performance notes, biographical sketches, and authentic matching audio with backing tracks.
00695586 Book/CD Pack.. $24.95

CHORD-MELODY
PHRASES FOR GUITAR

by Ron Eschete • REH ProLessons Series

Expand your chord-melody chops with these outstanding jazz phrases! This book covers: chord substitutions, chromatic movements, contrary motion, pedal tones, inner-voice movements, reharmonization techniques, and much more. Includes standard notation and tab, and a CD.
00695628 Book/CD Pack.. $17.99

CHORDS FOR JAZZ GUITAR
THE COMPLETE GUIDE TO COMPING,
CHORD MELODY AND CHORD SOLOING • *by Charlton Johnson*

This book/audio pack will teach you how to play jazz chords all over the fretboard in a variety of styles and progressions. It covers: voicings, progressions, jazz chord theory, comping, chord melody, chord soloing, voice leading and many more topics. The audio offers 98 full-band demo tracks. No tablature.
00695706 Book/Online Audio $19.95

FRETBOARD ROADMAPS –
JAZZ GUITAR
THE ESSENTIAL GUITAR PATTERNS
THAT ALL THE PROS KNOW AND USE • *by Fred Sokolow*

This book will get guitarists playing lead & rhythm anywhere on the fretboard, in any key! It teaches a variety of lead guitar styles using moveable patterns, double-note licks, sliding pentatonics and more, through easy-to-follow diagrams and instructions. The online audio includes 54 full-demo tracks.
00695354 Book/Online Audio $15.99

JAZZ IMPROVISATION FOR GUITAR
by Les Wise • REH ProLessons Series

This book/audio will allow you to make the transition from playing disjointed scales and arpeggios to playing melodic jazz solos that maintain continuity and interest for the listener. Topics covered include: tension and resolution, major scale, melodic minor scale, and harmonic minor scale patterns, common licks and substitution techniques, creating altered tension, and more! Features standard notation and tab, and online audio.
00695657 Book/Online Audio $17.99

JAZZ RHYTHM GUITAR
THE COMPLETE GUIDE
by Jack Grassel

This book/CD pack will help rhythm guitarists better understand: chord symbols and voicings, comping styles and patterns, equipment, accessories and set-up, the fingerboard, chord theory, and much more. The accompanying CD includes 74 full-band tracks.
00695654 Book/CD Pack.. $19.95

JAZZ SOLOS FOR GUITAR
LEAD GUITAR IN THE STYLES OF TAL FARLOW,
BARNEY KESSEL, WES MONTGOMERY, JOE PASS, JOHNNY SMITH
by Les Wise

Examine the solo concepts of the masters with this book including phrase-by-phrase performance notes, tips on arpeggio substitution, scale substitution, tension and resolution, jazz-blues, chord soloing, and more. The audio includes full demonstration and rhythm-only tracks.
00695447 Book/Online Audio $19.99

100 JAZZ LESSONS
Guitar Lesson Goldmine Series
by John Heussenstamm and Paul Silbergleit

Featuring 100 individual modules covering a giant array of topics, each lesson includes detailed instruction with playing examples presented in standard notation and tablature. You'll also get extremely useful tips, scale diagrams, and more to reinforce your learning experience, plus audio featuring performance demos of all the examples in the book!
00696454 Book/Online Audio $24.99

101 MUST-KNOW JAZZ LICKS
A QUICK, EASY REFERENCE GUIDE
FOR ALL GUITARISTS • *by Wolf Marshall*

Here are 101 definitive licks, plus demonstration audio, from every major jazz guitar style, neatly organized into easy-to-use categories. They're all here: swing and pre-bop, bebop, post-bop modern jazz, hard bop and cool jazz, modal jazz, soul jazz and postmodern jazz. Includes an introduction, tips, and a list of suggested recordings.
00695433 Book/Online Audio $17.99

SWING AND BIG BAND GUITAR
FOUR-TO-THE-BAR COMPING IN THE STYLE OF
FREDDIE GREEN • *by Charlton Johnson*

This unique package teaches the essentials of swing and big band styles, including chord voicings, inversions, substitutions; time and groove, reading charts, chord reduction, and expansion; sample songs, patterns, progressions, and exercises; chord reference library; and online audio with over 50 full-demo examples. Uses chord grids – no tablature.
00695147 Book/Online Audio $19.99

HAL•LEONARD®

Visit Hal Leonard Online at **www.halleonard.com**

*Prices, contents and availability
subject to change without notice.*